The map

Everyone is back at the house.
They are happy because now they have all the bits from the map.
The bits all fit.
The fuzzbuzzes have stuck them to some blue cloth.
Now they can see the full map.
Can you see it?

Draw the map.
Write
Now they have the full map.

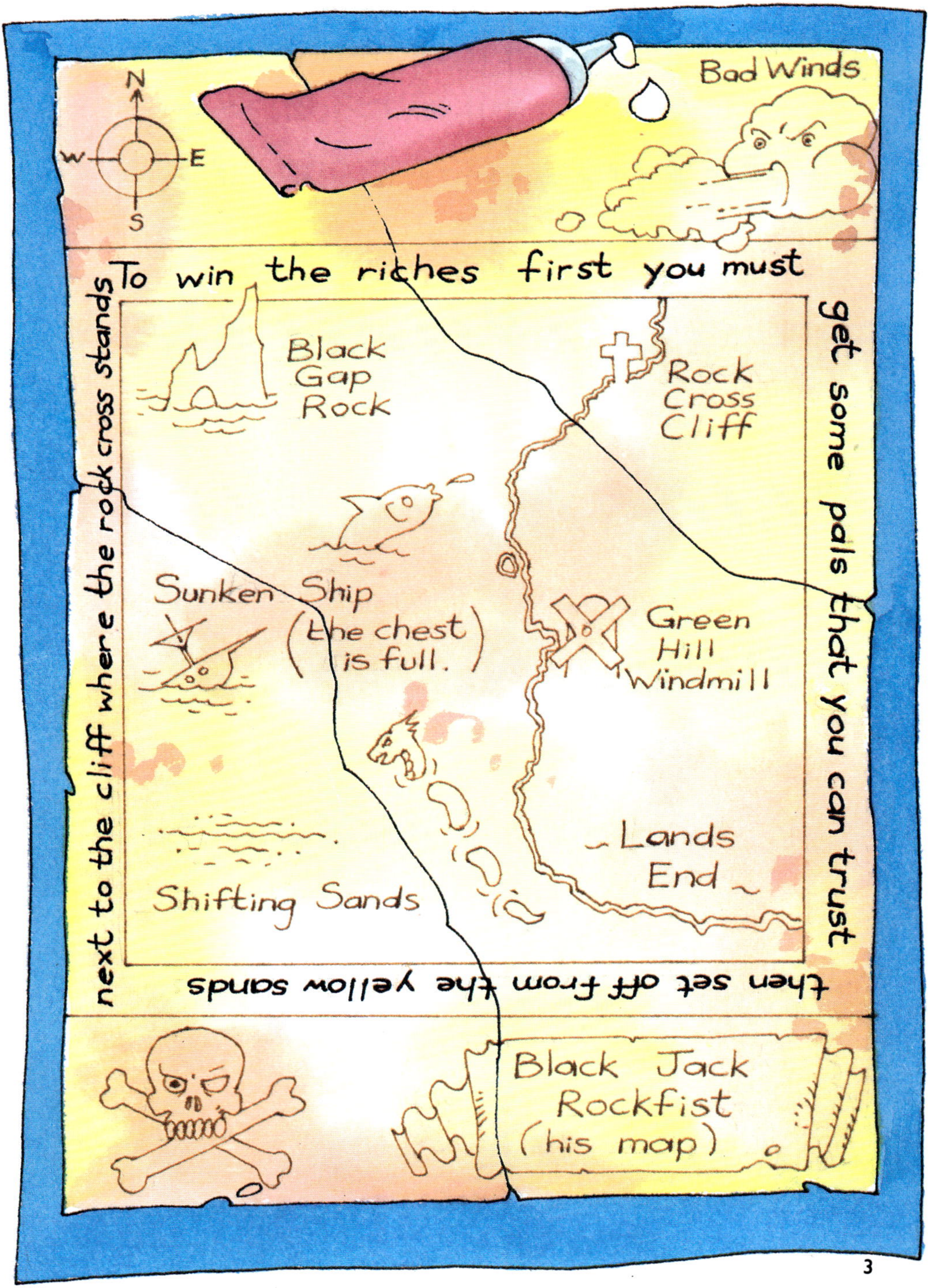
N
W
E
S
Bad Winds
To win the riches first you must
get some pals that you can trust
then set off from the yellow sands
next to the cliff where the rock cross stands
Black Gap Rock
Rock Cross Cliff
Sunken Ship
(the chest is full.)
Green Hill Windmill
Lands End
Shifting Sands
Black Jack Rockfist (his map)

They can see that getting to the sunken ship is a difficult job.
They must have a plan, and they must collect a lot of things for the trip.
Eggin writes a list of the things they must get.

Draw some of the things they will collect for the trip.

basket full of
good things to eat
chisel
mallet
lifting kit
frogman kit
brass helmet
gas tanks
big boots
plastic bin sacks
compass
string
big net
sleeping bags

mend the van

put a metal rack on top

get some tins of petrol

fix up a raft

collect everything

pack everything in

Now Eggin gives everyone a job to do.
Everyone must stick at it.
They must finish everything as fast as they can.
The end of summer is coming.
Then the winds and the frost will come.
They will not get to the sunken ship if that happens.
Everyone gets down to it.

Eggin and the Slinx are going to fix the van.
This is a very difficult job.
The van is just a lot of scrap.
It has rusted.
There are a lot of bits missing.

Eggin thinks that they will have to
give up.
Then the Slinx thinks of a
brilliant plan.
He gets a band of fuzzbuzzes.
He tells them that they must get
all the missing bits.
They must go to the biggest
dump in the land.
They will get all the
bits from there.
The fuzzbuzzes tell the Slinx that
they will do a good job.
The Slinx gives them a
shopping list.
Eggin gives them some cash.
They set off.

At last the little band of fuzzbuzzes come back.
They have got all the things.
The men from the biggest dump in the land have given them a lift.
They unpack the things.
Can you see the things on the truck?

Draw all the things.
Write
These are the things the fuzzbuzzes have collected.
Now they can fix the van.

The Slinx inspects everything.
He thinks that some of the things will not fit.
Can you see them?
The Slinx gets cross.
He snatches the list from the fuzzbuzzes.
He reads it.
Then he yells out—
'We forgot to write down how big the things are!
This is a mini-van.
These things are for a big truck!
Now what can we do?'

Write

The Slinx is cross.
Some of the things will not fit.
Draw the things.

The fuzzbuzzes are sad.
But Eggin tells everyone to sit down.
'We must not let every little problem stop us,' he tells them.
'If we do, we can give up now.
Let's just get on with the job, and see what happens.'
The fuzzbuzzes grin, but the Slinx is still grumpy.
'Come on, you lot,' Eggin yells.
'Let's get cracking.'
They all jump up, and go across to the van.
The Slinx goes with them.
In less than ten seconds, everyone is mending the van.

Draw everyone mending the van.

At last the van is mended.
Can you see it?
Some of the fuzzbuzzes are
just finishing it.
They are rubbing and scrubbing and
waxing and polishing it.
Now the van is spick and span.
The bits are not an exact fit.
But everyone thinks the van
will go.

Draw the mended van.
Write
This is the van.
The fuzzbuzzes have mended it and
given it a good polish.

polish

Now the Slinx comes.
Can you see what he has on?
He is going to give the van a test run.
Eggin brings a can of petrol and a funnel.
He fills the petrol tank.
Now everything is ready.
Will the van go?

Draw the Slinx.

Write

The Slinx loves to dress up.
He intends to give the van a test run.
Will it go?

Everyone gets in.
The Slinx switches on.
BRRUMM! BRRUMM!
The van goes at the first attempt!
Everyone is happy.
They go for a spin across the dump.
Then the Slinx presses down on the pedal.
The van goes fast.
They are not so happy now.
They think they will crash.
They all yell at the Slinx.

Draw the van going across the dump.

Write

The van goes fast and the fuzzbuzzes panic.

We will crash!
Stop!
Help!

At last the van comes to a stop.
Everyone gets out.
They tell the Slinx off.
He must not go so fast.
If he goes fast on the trip,
he will get arrested.
The Slinx tells them he will have
some more goes in the van first.
Then they can test him.
He gets back into the van.
Eggin sticks something on the back.
Can you see what it is?
Now the van goes well.
The Slinx sticks at it.
In the end he passes the test.

Draw what Eggin sticks on the van.

Write

The Slinx passes the test.

L

There are still some jobs
left to do.
First the metal rack has to go on
top of the van.
It must fit well.
The rack must not slip as there are
a lot of things to go on top.
Eggin checks all the nuts.

These fuzzbuzzes are doing the packing.
Everything must fit in.

Write
Everyone gets on with the rest of the jobs.

The Slinx has a big job to do.
He has got some tree trunks and logs, some planks, some string and some tins.
He is fixing them all up.
Some of the fuzzbuzzes come.
The Slinx is glad of the help.
It is a difficult job.
The Slinx gets very hot.
There is a lot to do.

Write

The Slinx and the fuzzbuzzes have a big job to do.

At last the job is ready.
Can you see what it is?
The Slinx is sad because they cannot test it yet.
He tells everyone that it will not sink.

Write
The last big job is ready.
The Slinx tells them it will not sink.
Draw it.

It will not sink

Now they must pack.
Lots of the things go in the van.
Lots of things go on top of it.
At last everything is ready.
The van is full up.
Now everyone can have a rest.
Eggin tells them that they must eat one last big dinner.
Then they must have a good sleep.
Then they will set off.
With a bit of luck, they will all get rich.
Everyone goes back to the house.

Write

The van is full up.
They will have a good sleep, then they will set off.

Draw the van with all the things.

L

1. Why is everyone happy? (2)
2. Why must they set off as fast as they can? (7)
3. Why is fixing the van a difficult job? (8)
4. What brilliant plan does the Slinx think of? (9)
5. Why does the Slinx get cross? (12)
6. What does the Slinx do to upset everyone? (20)
7. What does he have to do next? (22)
8. What big job does the Slinx do? (28)
9. Why do you think he cannot test it yet? (28)
10. What is the last job they all do? (30)